T... Country I've Been Dead In

R. Nikolas Macioci

With love to my brother, Michael, who always stands beside me
through the best and the worst

Acknowledgements

Clark Street Review—Visit to My Father After His Gunshot Wound

The Ballad of Broken Parents

A Fable of Final Effort

Chiron Review—Night Map to My Father

Tipton Poetry Journal—The Only Country I've Been Dead In

Contents

DISRUPTING THE CALM OF THEIR WORLD

When I nestled on my mother's lap,
she read Grimm's Fairy Tales and nursery
rhymes, covering dark forests and troll-guarded
bridges. I curved my body into hers, protected
from witches and wolves. She read children's
poetry, tapping out rhythms on a wooden,
rocking- chair arm. Without saying it,
we waited for the smokey breath of my
father to stumble through the door and destroy
our peaceful space.

All the books in the world couldn't save us
from his brutal approach, so we attempted
to sneak past him in a moment when he
teetered on unsteady feet. His hand
blocked us like a railroad signal. He grabbed
my mother's arm, pushing her back into
the rocking chair, while reprimanding me
for being in the way. I clutched my books
and bunched myself into a corner, pleading
him to stop. He haulted me by uncoiling
his black belt from its loops. Scared, books
dropped, and one of them fell open to "The
Peasant and the Devil." Because it was hard
to find a way past him, we waited until he tired
and fell asleep on the couch, his cigarette burning
a hole in the cushion.

THE BALLAD OF BROKEN PARENTS

I grew up and out of my mother's arms,
but they were there when I contracted
Rheumatic Fever, Scarlet Fever, and
a mastoid. They held me during Grimm's
Fairy Tales and traditional nursery rhymes,
She carried me nine months and was sick
every day. While my dad would have
given the proverbial shirt off his back,
he was the abusive one. Congenial
throughout the week, he transformed into
a drunken Hyde on weekends, physically
harmful to her, threatening to me.

Did I love my parents? Mom knew it. Dad
had to guess. On Barthman Avenue, I
slept in the room next to them and could
hear dangerous romance. Through paper-thin
walls, I listened to intermittent struggles
to stay married. The old-fashioned radio
program, *Moonriver,* accompanied intimacy.

After the divorce, my dad begged me to
visit him. He tried to entice me with
money and trinkets. Sometimes I went.
Something told me he didn't love me
except on the occasional greeting card.
I never kept any of them.

DAD, THE JUGGLER

Dad was not a professional juggler,
but he threw me in the air when I was six-
weeks- old and never caught me. Mom says
my head hit the hardwood floor. Obviously
I lived, but a slight dent in my head proves
the story. She said he had been drinking
all day, grabbed me from her and threw me
in the air. I guess I'm lucky I didn't end up
in a coffin or with a cracked-open skull.
As I grew older, he dropped me in other ways.
Two photographs depict him and me
before distance opened between us.

In the first one, we are dressed in Federal Glass
baseball outfits. Dad sits on grass near the diamond.
I stand between his legs, his arms wrapped
around me. I am a year old and too young
to remember his embrace.

In the second photograph, I am newborn,
and he is cradling me in the crook of his arm
as if someone had just shown him how
to hold a baby.

Soon after I learned to walk, I begin to feel
I wasn't going to be the son he wanted.
I don't know how I could have been so young
and figured that out, but I remember falling
asleep many nights feeling fatherless. Maybe

his drinking made him see me as unspecial
and ordinary. I don't think he loved me,
and I feared to go deep enough to find out
if I loved him.

TEDDY BEAR

To have a birthday on April Fool's Day
is to ask for weeping. I squared five-year-old
shoulders and picked up my last present,
a box wrapped in blue paper with a blue
ribbon. My parents had already given
me a red, Radio Flyer wagon and a toy
steam shovel. What could they have possibly
saved until last? Relatives in the room
watched me rip paper from the box and open
its flaps. I roughly removed tissue paper
to reveal a brown teddy bear exactly like
the one I already owned. Turning from
the box, gloriously happy to have two
identical bears, I began searching
for my old one. I looked on my bed, lay
on my stomach and fanned an arm beneath
the bed. I rummaged through my toy box
and everywhere it might be, but I couldn't find
the other bear. All the while, I clutched
the new bear to my chest and continued
to hunt. Finally, feeling defeated, I returned
to the room where my relatives waited.
When I entered, a chorus of voices roared out
"April Fool." I had carried the original
bear with me on my long journey of
disappointment. I learned that day about
distress from wanting more than I already had,
how sometimes secrecy can lead to tears.

NIGHT MAP TO MY FATHER

I am seven and locked in a car.
Afraid and needing to use the bathroom,
I consider choices, roll down a window
and climb through. Urgent to relieve myself,
I hurry along Parsons Avenue, not certain
which direction is right. I hustle onward,
orange and red leaves a haphazardly sewn quilt
under my feet. Streetlights are miniature moons
casting an eerie glow over frosted foliage.
I round the corner, not lost anymore.

Red reflections from a blinking Budweiser
sign flash redundant blood spots
on the sidewalk. The saloon door
has many cracks from years of sun's claw
marks. I twist the handle and enter. Smoke
is thick like a real cloud has been stuffed
into a single room. Dad bends at the bar,
a willow branch curved toward beer.
I tap him on the shoulder. He half turns
towards me, blurry-eyed as if looking through
dirty windows. He appears unsurprised
to see I have escaped from the car.
His slurred recognition digs into a pocket
and retrieves a fistful of crumpled bills
that I stuff into my pocket. He gives
no sign that I should return to the car,
so I grab the doorknob, push back
into the night, counting on a sense
of inner direction to find home.

KICK THE CAN

It's 1949 and after dark.
Very few cars cross the intersection
of Hinman and Bruck. I am eight years old,
and six of us neighborhood boys are playing
Kick the Can in the middle of the street.
The streetlight hangs over the intersection
like the bright eye of a watchdog. I kick,
and the silver can clatters across the street
and clangs into a curb. Just then, the front
door of our house bangs open, and the drunken
shadow of my dad staggers down the front
steps to the sidewalk. He's walking as fast
as he can without stumbling. Halfway to me,
I see his brown, leather belt has been pulled
from his pants and waggles in his hand like
a poisonous snake. I try to bolt toward
the house, but his hand holds me in place,
and he's cussing about my curfew. His belt
catches me on the back of my legs which
sting like alcohol on an open wound.
The belt continues to thrash my legs, bottom,
and back. It feels as if he really means to kill
me. We stutter up porch steps, and he's still
lashing me. In the house, he doesn't stop
until Mom hears my howling and races
from the kitchen to rescue me, but I'm
already crying at my bedroom window:
five boys still play the game, unburned
by their dads. They still sweep the can
from foot to foot.

VILLAGE

My eight-year-old hands dig dirt to shape
miniature roads. I route out imaginary
avenues away from Dad's threats with
guns and knives. On my knees between
stone piles, I construct a gas station from
sticks, a store from slices of stone. I make
a village where nothing bad can happen,
where Dad cannot tie me in a chair and
force me to eat meat. My eyes blur when
I remember belt marks on the backs of my legs,
but I keep building this small town where
imagination lives for temporary escape.

Most of the day, I do not return to the house
because I know his routine of swigging beer
on weekends. That is when his civility fades,
and I am caught in the eye of his personal
storm. That is when he corners me with his
finger on the trigger or the flash of a blade.

By dusk, I'm late for supper and will brave
consequences, but I must finish the village,
put final touches on a safe environment
where make-believe people do not get drunk
and give rise to dangerous behavior.

PRACTICE

My dad pitched a mean baseball
for Federal Glass. Truth surfaced early
that I had no interest in learning to play.

Once, he prodded me into the backyard
for toss and catch. He had a short, compact
body, hence the nickname, Shorty, whereas
I was thin as a spurious excuse.

He wound up. I failed to shift forward
fast enough and missed the ball by several feet.
"Get out of the yard, if you can't play," he yelled.
I slumped into the house. He followed, uncapped
a beer, insisted I threw like a girl.

From my room I heard Sunday baseball drift
up from the living room radio.
He knew how to play ball and how to love
a woman.

I go on afraid to pitch, afraid to love.
My dad is dead now, and, for me, it just keeps
snowing on his grave.

SUPPERTIME

I remember bad times at the table.
Mom dished mashed potatoes onto my plate
while Dad's eyes burned to reprimand me
or whip out his belt which had many times
licked my legs like a monster's leather tongue.

On this particular night, I had come
to the table without shoes, had been
warned never to come to dinner shoeless.
We were a casual family, but he had been
drinking heavily and was looking for
someone to pick on. He and Mom begin
to argue. My eight-year-old mind did not
grasp their disagreement. He slammed his dish
of food against the wall, went into the bedroom,
reappeared with a gun. He aimed it at Mom.
She began to whimper and plead. I jumped
off my chair, wedged myself between them.
He turned quicker than a dervish and shot
three holes in the linoleum floor. He returned
to the bedroom for something. We raced from
the kitchen, through the front door, down
twenty steps, and up the alley where we hid
behind our building until a neighbor let us
use a phone to call Mom's sister.

We camped out at Aunt Ada's for two days
until he sobered up and called, beseeching
us to come home.

When my aunt and uncle dropped us off,
we climbed those twenty steps and found him
passed out on the couch with the first
of many gambrinus bottles beside him.

HINMAN AVENUE

Dad is perched on the top step of the front
porch. His beer belly pushes over his belt.
He wears s sleeveless undershirt, no shoes,
no socks. Shoving the nightly newspaper
aside, he stands and beckons me to him.
I'm nine and on the lawn shoving a push
mower, its reels spitting out grass. He
touches his belt, but doesn't unfasten it.
"Your mom says you were at the neighbors.
She didn't know where you were." His
hand is still on his belt. Smell of fried
potatoes wafts through the screen door.
I'm shirtless, July sun fiery on my shoulders.
I stand there condemned, waiting for him
to tear his belt from the loops, "Don't go
anywhere without telling your mom." I
wonder if this is a reprieve or a prelude
to punishment. Just then, Mom appears
at the screen door to announce supper is
ready. He stands, hands at his sides.
"After supper, finish the grass." Turning
away from me, he enters the house. I
park the mower beside the porch and follow
him in. The screen door slams shut, and
I apologize for not catching it in time.

THE KINGDOM OF EMPTY HEARTS

At night, I see Dad beneath my eyelids
holding Mom at knifepoint. I expect dreams
to drag me away from a bank book burned
in the middle of the breakfast table, gunshot
holes popped through kitchen floor.

I want to rise from bed and ask my parents
to name their troubles, so I can help. As a
ten- year-old, I am ready to undertake the task.
Unable to sleep, I watch shadows splash
walls from cars passing down Barthman
Avenue, my greatest fear that they will die
without ever having said they love me.

Too awake to sleep, I rise and look out
a window at midnight traffic, watch for
one of their cars to pull up to the curb,
worried that they have been in an accident.

I pace back and forth, occasionally
counting cars to occupy myself. Around two
in the morning, a pair of headlights coast
to a stop, and Mom climbs stairs to our
apartment. Dad has disappeared for the night,
likely spending it in another woman's bedroom.
I conclude this from previous suspicions
of his infidelity. I would like to ask him
to be only with Mom, but I am just
a kid awakened by something beyond my
comprehension, something I do not wish
to know more about.

THE LAWS OF EXCLUSION

I was reared on isolation, a child
slender and dreaming of protection.
I gave life to plastic soldiers and
circus performers on the ledge of
the Philco console radio. Even then,
I knew I couldn't make it through
days without imagination, so while
listening to *The Lone Ranger*, I changed
the whereabouts of the figures to a
circle of sun on a flowered carpet.

Then one pre-teen Sunday afternoon,
when I thought I'd rot away from boredom,
following a mashed potato-roast beef-parents-
bickering routine, I left the house and
walked a dozen blocks to the Russell theater,
dropped myself into a seat, watched
lights dim on the beginning of escape.

Film clicked through the projector and
made a world where a poet was born,
a world where I slowly drifted away
from a dysfunctional family and let
words off the screen become my
dialogue with make-believe and loneliness.

CARNIVAL

My nine-year-old eyes search dark sky for clues
that a carnival has spread itself out
on the empty lot beside the bank. Doubt
evaporates when a spotlight tattoos
clouds with its whereabouts. Eager, I choose
familiar alleys, certain of my route,
and race to find the Ferris wheel about
eight blocks from home. Excited with the news,
I hunt for Dad in a neighborhood bar
where cigarette smoke has eaten the air
like an invisible monster. I plead
with him the carnival is not so far,
then watch his tipsy hand that doesn't care
reach into pockets to hush up my need.

ON BARTHMAN AVENUE

Mom is the landlord of an apartment
over our confectionery on Barthman
Avenue. A man has just moved out.
She says how hard it is to find a reliable
tenant. Mom and her sister, Liz, are cleaning
his residence. I help as much as I can.
Like Hercules, our labors are many:
scour the stove, scrub the refrigerator,
clean toilets, wash walls. We work
into the night, tireless as Sisphus.

Their German roots demand a beer
at finish, so we slog downstairs
to the confectionery. An open bottle
under the counter, Dad has already
had a few: not sodden yet, but glary-eyed.
I've become adept at foreseeing
trouble between my parents and walk home.

I am a nine-year-old boy who collects
loose change. My dad never gets closer than his
handout to me. By the time they drop
Aunt Liz off and arrive home, I am
lying in bed waiting for the crash
of dishes or a random gunshot. Mom
pulls me out of bed, and we hurry
to someplace safe. He follows, but we hide
until he tramps back home, passes out.

OLD-FASHION DISCIPLINE 1948

It was during those days that a Dad could whip
his son with guaranteed impunity,
and among the worldwide community
of fathers, they would have thought right to strip
a belt from loops and thus begin the nip
and run routine. It was useless to flee.
In my case, he always caught up with me,
and I took it without giving him lip.
There has to be fear in discipline, some
sense that something will be taken away:
dignity, possessions, time. Without rules
the road is too wide, and many will turn
into the ditch. My dad showed me a way.
Without common laws we all become fools.

SMOKE

Dad is six feet behind the foul line,
back straight as a rose stem, fourteen
pound ball raised in both hands like
a primitive sacrifice. He aims, starts
his approach, begins his swing
into an arc that coasts the ball
onto the alley. His smooth delivery
clobbers the pins, and the strike triggers
congratulatory shouts from his teammates.

My nine-year-old lungs are tangled
in cigarette smoke, nerves edgy to be
out of there. On this particular night,
Mom has relegated me to Dad's bowling
mania, and he has relegated me to a
hardwood bench in the back of the alley.
I'm given a pop and instructions not to go
elsewhere. Fidgety by nature, I feel
trapped between tar exhalations and the
crash of pins against one another.

When the games are finished, Dad, gasping
a little, sweaty as a wrestler, herds me
into the barroom up front, and I am trapped
again, my imagination measuring the distance
home. After his fourth beer, my knees are cramped,
and I'm angry that I've fallen into his care.

He back slaps buddies and baits waitresses
with bravado. Sleepy, I lay my head on the table.
It's late when I follow him out the door, buried
in his stench of smoke.

VISIT TO MY FATHER AFTER HIS GUNSHOT WOUND

After my parents' divorce, Dad rents
a room from his sister on South 5th Street.
A gold crucifix hangs above his bed,
and a dusty arrangement of dried wildflowers
bulges out of a chipped vase on a side table.
Stains pockmark beige wallpaper. The blind
is pulled down on the single window,
summer escaping in yellow strips across
threadbare carpet. The rebellious debris of
cigarette butts and ash overflows
an ashtray on a bedside table.

On the bed he lies naked and passed out,
snoring like a sow. I shake his shoulder,
and he groans awake, his breath alive with beer.
He sits up, his feet on the floor, and tells me
about being shot the previous week.
A horizontal incision runs across
his stomach, around to his back, and up
to his shoulder. In spite of stitches,
the entire incision gaps like the gill
opening on a shark.

He is partial to women in bars, and
his most recent fling is with someone
who packs a gun. He lies back on the bed
and lights a cigarette. Without anger
for the way he has abused my life,

I leave, descending dark stairs at the end
of which hangs another crucifix
flaming in sunset from a side window
like a sign of sobering reassurance.

AN ISOLATED PLACE

The reverberative honking from a V
formation of geese draws my attention
upward as I crunch steps over field
stubble and away from the pond in
the middle of Welch's Woods. Ice
skates hang over my twelve-year-old
shoulder. Their blades catch white
reflections of an early January moon
and the gray of dusk. There is no one
to speak to. My eyes search for an
incidental companion.

A hundred yards ahead, I can see
my house. Lamp light from the
living room window throws a path
over a dusting of snow. The yellow
glow of warmth conjures an image
of love within, but that is a midwinter
illusion. Divorce lives there and the
brutality of separated parents.

I arrive at the front door, stop and
realize I don't want to go in anymore.
I want to return to the woods and skate
under the stars until I am weary.

THE ONLY COUNTRY I'VE BEEN DEAD IN

One night I hope to find you in a dream,
to learn what a father's embrace is
and finally resolve the pain of a flawed
relationship. Because I saw you naked
so many times sleeping off a bender,
I knew your body and its scars. I sat
beside the bed and believed, though
it may have been thin as bone, that
you loved me. Even if you had awakened
and nagged me not to be your child,
I would have waited to hear it from God.
I would have waited to make sense
of the passionate waiting, to know why
I wouldn't just close the door on your
vacancy. I huddled down in that room,
hugged my knees, believing someone cared
about my solitude. I thought you had
abandoned me again this time in sleep.
The crucifix above your bed looked
too heavy for a nail to hold. Palm fronds
hung behind it. I gazed at you in terror
that you would open your eyes and not see
me. I heard you snore, watched your chest
move with boozy breathing. The brass
Jesus gleamed. Jerusalem had never been
so close.

THE DIVINE BITTERNESS OF DISEN-CHANTMENT

My dad did not know how to love,
even though his body slipped into
Mom's bed and sweetened the night
with sex. I can count on no hands the times
I saw them kiss. If I had given my heart
to him, he would have been witty about
taking it which would have translated as not
having taken it at all. Intelligent people

have no trouble with numbers, and I saw
him more than once tally a column of
integers in seconds. It seems I had no chance
against those numbers to be added in.

Mom and I kept our distance from his sporadic
violence and tendency to hurt. Mom's effort to
protect me did not keep me from being damaged.

This poem is a tongue that tells
the truth about my grieving for love, about
being alone, about wondering through the
reasons why the world went on without me.

ITALIAN MILIEU

Dad would take a butcher knife, slice
a whole loaf of Italian bread in half
horizontally and make a single sandwich.
Behind him, his sister, Aunt Mary Simmons,
stirred a kettle of homemade spaghetti sauce
that boiled and popped like red lava.
She always kept a canary, round and yellow
as an egg yolk, in a cage by the window,
it's peep, peep, peep persisted throughout the day.

Dad was sober during these hours
when I would come down from our apartment
in the next-door building, visit with him
and take in as much old world Italian
atmosphere as my twelve-year-old mind
could absorb.

He quipped, joked, or uttered witticisms.
He never gave a straight answer to a question.
The whole neighborhood loved his generosity,
affability. His nickname was Shorty,
and he became a kind of icon of the South End.
I puffed up with pride when I walked
down the street with him because almost
everyone we passed applauded his presence.

On weekends, however, the dark demon
of drink usurped his personality,
set his mean streak on autopilot. He would

either go next door and threaten Mom or
climb his sister's stairs and sleep off the bender
in the spare room. Sometimes, I sat on the floor
beside his bed, watched him snore, and studied
the crucifix above his headboard as if waiting
for Jesus to come down from the cross and explain
alcoholism.

ICICLES

In childhood, our Christmas tree was huge
and shimmered icicles. I was not allowed
to decorate the tree and especially not
allowed to drape icicles. Mom lay each
strand perfectly, so that it draped down
like a tear on a cedar cheek. Back then,
in the 50s and 60s, icicles were made
from real aluminum not plastic or any
other synthetic material. When tree lights
were on, icicles glittered. When tree lights
were off, icicles coruscated the length of
the tree like a silver falls. As a child
I spent some time, staring at the unlit tree,
thinking it beautiful even without bulbs burning.
Today, I see only plastic, thread-like fibers,
dull as dirty mirrors, barely reflecting light,
their subdued rainbow shine as unprepossessing
as an oil spill.

Three days ago, in the main lobby of the art
museum in Lancaster, Ohio, I saw my
childhood Christmas tree again. An immense
evergreen showered in old-fashioned,
aluminum icicles caught the afternoon
sun from windows on either side. I half closed
my eyes and stepped back, squinting into
the past and saw a staircase leading down to
Mom meticulously draping each icicle into
place before Dad stumbled through the door,

tossed a handful of icicles on the tree, rebuked
her, then dropped to sleep on the sofa, bedecked
in alcohol and indifference.

NEW YEAR'S EVE, 1947

His hand extends from the cuff of his starched,
white shirt, grabs me by the forearm, presses me
through the house and down basement steps.
What have I done wrong but weep for my parents'
departure on New Year's Eve? My dad, handsome
as Valentino, has lost patience with me. I have
disobeyed his command to be silent. Ethel, the
babysitter, has not yet arrived before he bolts me
into the boxed-in area of the basement where only
coal belongs. My eyes seek light in the bottomless
dark. The search starts at the drop of a latch on the
coalbin door. My six-year-old face feels made of
tears as I hear my dad's steps ascending stairs to the
kitchen. Like coal, I become disposable, and like
coal, I become another piece of the blackness that
surrounds me. In her bedroom, I know Mom preens
at her dresser, oblivious to what is happening below.
Above my head, indistinguishable radio sounds of
the *Grand Ole Opry* reassure me that my parents
have not left. My skull aches to see a reference point,
a pinpoint of light. I place my hands in front of me
and cannot find them. Unlike my heart, the dark is
unbroken. Hope disintegrates, and new tears replace
old ones. I think I have no friend in the world when
finally the lock clicks open, and he stands there
in white shirt, flowered tie, and green cufflinks.
I slide past him and race upstairs, thinking, within
my most secret self, if only I could be free of this
particular Dad, I would promise God anything.

CIRCUS

When I was a kid, circuses were in tents
not indoor arenas. One major tent,
the size of a small stadium, housed aerial
riggs and three, raised rings in which
performers presented their acts. Ringling
Brothers, Barnum & Bailey hoisted their
tent in a vacant field next to Red Bird Stadium.

Memory compels me to talk about the bar
across the street from the circus where dad drank
his fourth beer while I fidgeted beside him.
Restless, I descended stairs to the restroom
in the basement. I was nine-years-old, and
everything about my life seemed wrong.
I stared into the mirror above the dirty sink,
wondering if I stared long enough I could
step into a different world where I wouldn't
be abused.

I went back upstairs and played the jukebox.
Doris Day's "Teacher's Pet" provided an upbeat
moment, and I imagined performing it
to an audience who fully accepted me.

After two more beers, we crossed the street
to the midway where he bought me a chameleon
on a short string with a small safety pin to attach it
to my shirt. The purchase gave me something to love,
something that needed me to take care of it.

When we boarded the bus home on Mound Street,
Dad slept, and I watched the neighborhood scroll by
as if it were on a paper roll. While he snored,
I felt safe from the volatile world in which
he held me prisoner.

SLEDDING

I'm puffing my breath against the window
in which Mom has hung velvet wreaths
each with a fake candle and a single red bulb.
She hangs the same wreaths every year in all
the first floor windows. It's two weeks before
Christmas, and she says the appropriate time
to decorate.

Outside, Hinman Avenue is covered
with six inches of snow that sparkles
like white sequins under the streetlight.
Because traffic is spare, kids sled back
and forth through the intersection of
Hinman and Sixth Street, their commotion
clearly heard in our living room. I turn
from the window, put on my coat, gloves,
and knitted hat. My sled is on the front
porch, and I grab it on the way down
the steps to the street.

The first thing I do is a belly slam through
the intersection. Snow flies into my face,
but to an eight-year-old, a face full of snow
is only a challenge to do another slam.
I romp like this for half an hour until a
shadow with a belt hanging at its side
darkens our porch. Even though I'm
sledding in front of the house, I left
without permission, and the punishment

will be welts on my legs. His first swing
feels twenty times worse than I expected.
The second and third are layered upon numbness.
Though I'm sure my friends hear my cries,
they continue to play sled tag, helpless
to run back between a drunken man and his son.
He opens the door and shoves me through.
Inside the house is dark except for the
blood-red glow from the wreaths.

SUPPERTIME, 1950

My dad sits on the front porch with bare feet,
toenails neatly trimmed. A cigarette hangs
from his lip, smells like burning leaves.
I'm perched on porch steps looking at him.
I have a habit of staring at him, thinking
it will help me to know him better if I study his
face. Even at age nine, I know he is handsome.
Black hair slicked back, his brown eyes look
nowhere in particular. We don't talk. It's as if
I were alone. I cannot answer my own question
about why he is my dad and not someone else.
Last night he was drunk and threatened to shoot
Mom. While they argued in the kitchen, I
hovered in the dining room afraid to move.
Mom rushed me out the door to her sister's
house where we hid under the dining room
table while he pounded fists on the front door.
My aunt called the police, and they subdued him.
That was yesterday. Today, Mom is back
in the kitchen frying pork chops and intimating
divorce but reluctant to carry through.
An open bottle of Gambrinus sits beside his chair.
The paperboy stops his bicycle on the sidewalk,
tosses the evening paper onto the porch. Dad
unfolds the paper to the sports page. During these
moments, life seems normal on Hinman Avenue,
and I am happy that he hasn't done anything
so far to make me cry. Between cigarettes and
gulps of beer, he orders me to get the push mower

from the garage and cut the front lawn. As I mow,
I get a whiff of pork chops, pretend our house
is a place of love and peace. At dinner he will
tie me to a chair and because I do not like meat,
force it down my throat.

DAD, NEVER A CLOSED CASE

When I was a little boy and had a sore throat,
Mom rubbed Vicks on it and wrapped a sock
around my neck. It always worked, or its
success was a coincidence to natural healing.
She knew many home remedies but
lacked one to rescue her ruined marriage.
I hid in the corners of rooms when my
parents argued, my tongue quiet, my mouth
furred with fear. Dad would back her against
the wall with intimidation and threats to her
life. I wanted to jump between them and
receive the abuse myself, but I was too small
to make a difference. My dad was a weekend
drunk, but at other times, a tireless worker
who had wrapped the neighborhood around
his affable personality and constant generosity.
When it came to a work ethic, Mom was more
than his equal. Together they made their
confectionery a booming business. His
alcoholism was the brown spot in the apple
of their success. I never did love my dad.
He wouldn't let me. He was the thorny tree
I couldn't get my arms around without injury,
so I stood back with my heart clogged with need.

As an adult I can only see so far behind
the scenes and will never know why he chose
to damage our lives.

DAD AT THE FOUNDRY

It had been years since I'd seen him.
This would be next to the last time.
He met me at the main gate, face lined
by years of hard living, shoulders sagged
from different Hells he's experienced.
In his early seventies, he lived with
his sister, Aunt Mary Simmons, on
S. Sixth Street. She had given me
his work address,.

Wherever he labored throughout his life,
he soon occupied a management position,
so I wasn't surprised to find him holding
a superintendent's job at the foundry
on Hosack Street.

Rumor had a woman in love with him
Later, I learned they had two boys. At least
my dad belonged to someone now.

When we shook hands at the main gate,
I didn't want to let go. Holiness
surfaced for those few seconds.

I walked to my car remembering
his final words,"Come see me sometime."
I was only a speck in his eye. He
wouldn't have known what I was talking about
if I'd told him I loved him.

A FABLE OF FINAL EFFORT

It's sundown when I arrive. Shadows along
the driveway are black flowers. I knock,
and my dad opens the door. It's been twenty
years since I've seen him. His Al Pacino
looks are gone: black hair white and thinned,
a prosthesis in his throat produces
a tiny and far away speaking voice.
His neck is flabby, his face dropped into
a gravity-ridden mask of itself.

We sit at the kitchen table. I seek
conversation topics. He interrupts
most of my words with quippy comments
and lame banter. It's clear I won't have
the heart-to-heart exchange I've wanted
all of my life.

His wife comes to the door, says hello, and leaves.
He asks me how I like my stepmother,
says he's writing a novel. As I watch him
I think this will be the last attempt I will ever make
to know him. I won't go near him again.

Several years later, someone sent me
his obituary. He was seventy-seven.
I put the clipping in my Bible. Years later
I couldn't find it, no matter how hard I looked.

www.ingramcontent.com/pod-product-compliance
Lightning Source LLC
LaVergne TN
LVHW041442170726
843492LV00008B/2750